SURPRISES IN MILI'S SUITCASE

How I Cured My Diabetes with Food

written by Katherine Orr & Antonia Demas, PhD
illustrated by Katherine Orr

This book is not intended to be a substitute for medical advice. Before starting any lifestyle change in diet or exercise, please consult with your physician or healthcare professional who can evaluate your individual physical condition and advise you about any special considerations.

© 2019 Katherine Orr and Antonia Demas, PhD
All Rights Reserved
No part of this book may be reproduced in any form or by any electronic or mechanical means including information storage and retrieval systems without permission in writing from the publisher, except by a reviewer who may quote brief passages in a review.

For information please contact
Antonia Demas, PhD
Food Studies Institute
30 Cayuga St. Trumansburg, NY, 14886
USA

Printed in USA

This book is dedicated to bringing
the Hawaiian spirit of aloha and mālama ʻaina
to children and adults everywhere.

In loving memory of Mildred "Mili" Pang

Foreword

When it comes to the health of our children, we are living in dangerous times. Childhood obesity has tripled during the last three to four decades, and many are justifiably concerned about where this problem is headed. One consequence is assured: an increased number of children with diabetes. So-called adult-onset diabetes (type 2), as the name implies, once was reserved for adults. Now, this disease is affecting younger and younger children, and it is no coincidence that it is also part of the upward trend in obesity.

Surprises in Mili's Suitcase, a beautiful little book intended for children, is really a very big story for people of all ages. Personally, I would love to see this book be read far and wide. It provides a very constructive message for all those children who have food-related health problems. It is exactly what is needed for today's children and their families.

Katherine Orr and Antonia Demas bring to this story a sincere appreciation of children and their abilities, along with a reliable knowledge about what creates health and prevents disease. As a team, their unique blend of skills in graphic arts and writing, combined with knowledge and experience of children, education, and nutrition, result in a book that is delivered in an easy-to-understand manner based on a health message about the healing power of food. As a bonus, I find this book to be an exceptionally caring and clever way to inform parents about a health solution for their children.

Katherine Orr is an accomplished children's book author and illustrator with many books to her credit. She is also a marine biologist and she holds a certificate in plant-based nutrition from eCornell and the T. Colin Campbell Center for Nutrition Studies. This book arose from her enthusiastic desire to use her knowledge to help improve lives.

I am pleased to say I have known Dr. Antonia Demas for many years. I was her graduate research nutrition advisor for her PhD degree in education at Cornell University, for which she received two national awards for excellence and creativity. I know of no one better equipped to bring this important message forward than Dr. Demas. She has had many years working with young school-age children, is the founder of a successful program for children in food literacy, and was the first professional to take this message to school lunch programs in the United States. She is the grand dame of food literacy education.

Both authors have dedicated their professional lives to improving the quality of life for children, for their families, and on the planet. This book should be in every pediatrician's office, school library, and home with school-age children.

—T. Colin Campbell, PhD, author of *The China Study*,
Professor Emeritus of Nutritional Biochemistry, Cornell University

From the bitterness of disease one learns the sweetness of health."
—Catalan proverb

"Food can say *aloha* in a million different ways." That's what Grandma Tutu always said. *Tutu* means grandparent in Hawaiian, and *aloha* means the spirit of loving kindness. Tutu's favorite thing was sharing loving gifts of food.

"When we celebrate, food can say, 'Well done!'" she explained. "When someone's hurting or sick, food can say, 'I hope you're feeling better.'"

We all knew food was a gift of love and caring, but a gift of health? Well, I never thought about it. At least not until the year I turned eleven. That was the year I got diabetes.

Mom said, "Diabetes is in our genes. Tutu has it, and so does your Uncle Kim. But you, Hana, are still so young." She hugged me and her eyes were sad. "I'll help you learn to live with diabetes."

And for a while she did just that—until Mom's sister, Mili, came to visit. She stayed for the summer and everything changed. Auntie Mili and the surprises in her suitcase showed me how to live *without* diabetes! Here's the way it happened.

When the doctor gave me the diagnosis, he explained diabetes like this:

After we eat, our blood sugar rises. Then *insulin* moves the sugar from our blood into our cells, where it is burned to give us the energy to run and play. When we have diabetes, insulin isn't doing its job. Too much sugar stays in the blood. The extra sugar causes big trouble and slowly makes us sick.

Then he dropped the bomb...

"You'll need to take medicine every day."

"For how long?" I asked.

"For the rest of your life," he replied.

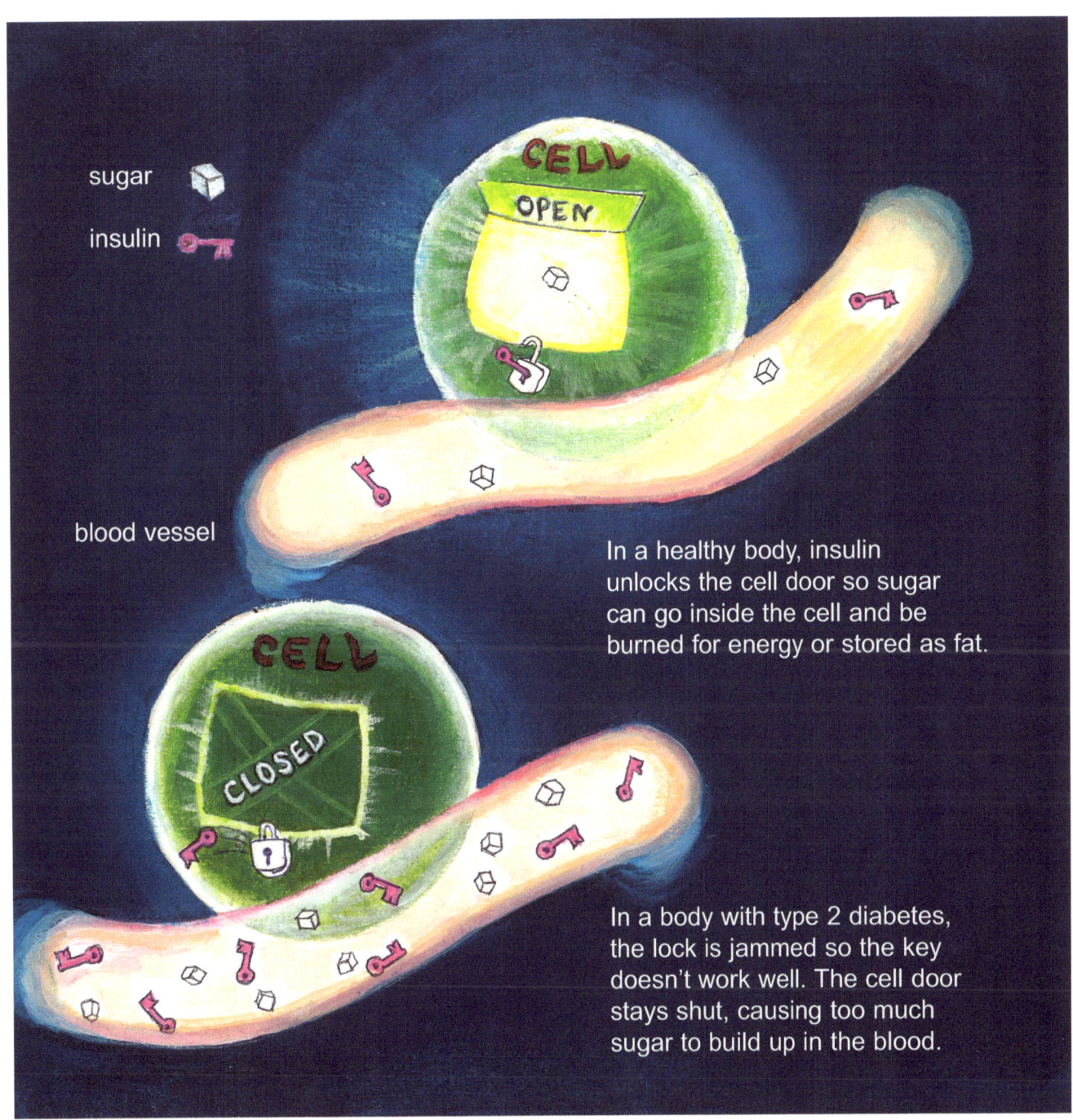

I was scared this meant sticking a needle in my skin. That's what Uncle Kim and Tutu did. But the doctor gave me pills instead. He said, "Eat right, lose weight, exercise, and get enough sleep. These things will help you manage your disease."

He gave Mom and me a booklet called *The Diabetes Diet*. It was full of instructions about counting carbs and calories, and it had lots of numbers that I didn't understand. But one thing was clear: if I didn't control my blood sugar I could wind up blind, or paralyzed from a stroke like my Uncle Kim. Or with leg and kidney problems like Tutu had.

I measured my blood sugar several times a day so the doctor would know how much medicine to give me. First I took a special strip and placed it in a meter. Next I pricked my finger to draw a drop of blood. Then I held the meter so the strip absorbed the blood, and the meter showed a number. That number told the level of sugar in my blood. I did this first thing every morning, and before and after every meal. At school I went to the nurses' office daily, where they kept a meter and did the blood test for me.

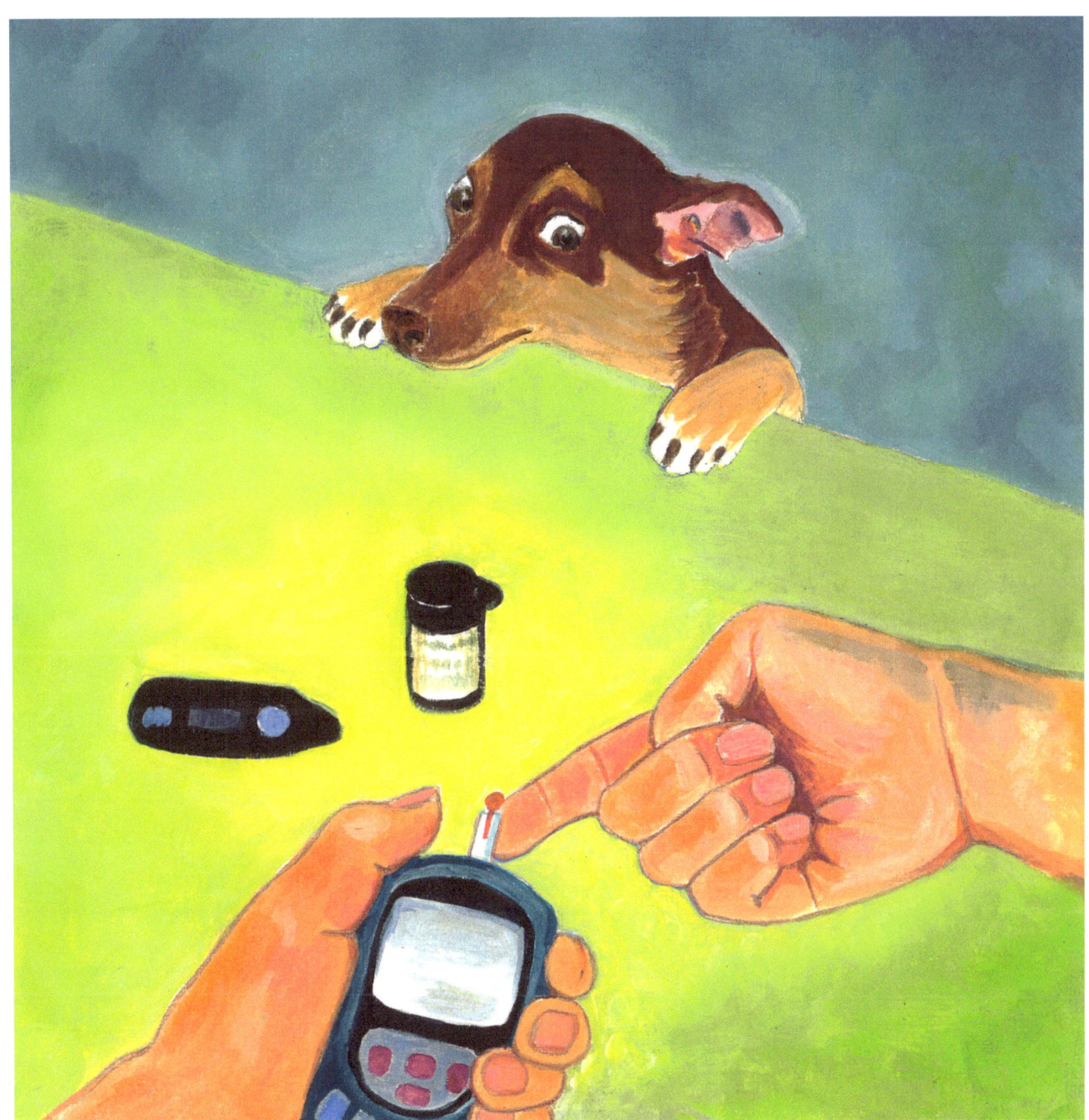

Some of my classmates were scared they might get sick, so my teacher explained diabetes wasn't catching. She said that what I have, called *type 2 diabetes*, used to be called *adult onset* diabetes because only grownups got it. But now the name has changed because so many children have it.

On the diabetes diet I was always watching what I ate. I ate steamed white chicken without the skin. I drank skim milk and ate low-fat cheese and yogurt. For snacks I drank diet soda, and my cookies were always sugar free. I tried to eat small meals, but the less I ate the more I was always thinking of food. I often felt tired and many times I didnt have the energy to play.

Summer vacation was just starting when Auntie Mili flew over from *Maui*. "Aloha!" she called, with her arms spread wide, waving humungous bags of food. Like Tutu, Auntie Mili saw food as a gift of love and caring. But her foods were different from the ones Tutu gave me.

Her suitcase was so heavy I could barely lift it. "What's *in* this thing?" I asked as I dragged it in the door.

"It's full of surprises!" she said with a grin. "Open it and see!"

As I lifted the lid, out spilled books, DVDs, some oranges and a carrot. "Did you bring stories and movies to make us laugh?" I asked.

Auntie Mili shook her head. "These books and DVDs are something much more special. They hold knowledge, Hana. Knowledge that can change your life and make you well again! The authors of these books and DVDs are scientists and doctors. They've uncovered a cure that's very exciting. They will help you understand about the awesome power of food."

"Oh, I know all about the awesome power of food," I said, gazing at the lemon cream cake sitting on the counter. It was a family favorite, and Mom's special gift to welcome Mili home.

"Ho! You're talking about the power of food *addiction*," said Auntie Mili. "Addictive foods taste so good that we want to keep eating them, but they're not good for our health. They are full of sugar, fat, salt, and chemicals. No, I'm talking about the awesome power of foods that can prevent diseases and even help heal them. I'm talking about the awesome power of *whole food plant-based nutrition*!"

"Whole food *what*?" I asked
"Whole food plant-based nutrition!" Mili said with a wink. "You see, your body knows how to make itself well, but it needs the right fuel to do it. Your type 2 diabetes came from eating foods that can harm your body. We need to focus on the foods that taste really good *and* make you strong, smart, and healthy."

Auntie Mili reached into her suitcase and pulled out another surprise. "A wise doctor named Hippocrates, who lived thousands of years ago in ancient Greece, said, 'Let food be your medicine, and medicine be your food.' He's called the father of modern medicine, but modern medicine has lost his message. Hana, eating whole foods from plants *is* the medicine that can make you well."

"What do you mean by *whole foods*?" I asked.

"Whole foods come from nature," Auntie Mili explained, "so they still have all their parts as nature grew them. They haven't had their ingredients rearranged or removed like *processed foods*, which come from a factory."

"We're following the diabetes diet," Mom said.

Auntie Mili shook her head and picked up a large carrot. "The doctors who recommend the diabetes diet have been trained to *manage* diabetes, not cure it. They've been taught to use drugs and do surgeries. Many doctors don't know about the surprises in my suitcase that teach us about the amazing healing power of whole foods." Auntie Mili waved the carrot as if brandishing a sword. "When it comes to healthy foods, nature knows best. My motto is, *Reach for the carrot instead of the cake!*"

The meals in *The Diabetes Diet* were what Auntie Mili called SAD. "They're just low-fat, low-sugar versions of the Standard American Diet," she said. "That's S.A.D. for short, and it's "sad" because it lacks the nutrition people need to stay healthy. It's full of processed foods. It's also full of animal foods, such as chicken, fish, eggs, yogurt, cheese, and milk."

Auntie Mili and the surprises in her suitcase explained why processed foods and animal foods were nutritionally poor choices that helped keep my body sick. "When factories make processed foods they usually remove healthy nutrients and add unhealthy chemicals to increase *shelf life*," she said. "Animal foods are life-saving when people are starving for calories, but they're lacking in certain nutrients people need from whole plants. And do you know, the food group that contains the highest percent of protein is not meat or dairy, but dark leafy greens? No wonder the biggest strongest animals on earth, like elephants and rhinos, thrive on eating plants!"

"And let's not forget about the soil," Mili continued. "We turn healthy food into junk food by removing nutrients and adding chemicals. We turn healthy soil into junk soil in the same way. Healthy soil is alive with *microbes*, worms, and other living things that need to be fed. When we add *compost* to soil, worms and microbes eat it and turn it into more soil. Can you guess why we sometimes call this soil 'black gold'?"

"Because its color is so lovely and dark?" I asked.

"Yes," said Aunty Mili, "and because it is so rich in *organic* nutrients that feed the plants. Rich soil, sun, and rain grow strong, healthy plants. When we eat these plants we grow strong and healthy, too! By nurturing our soil and caring for our land we are also caring for ourselves and each other. We are practicing the tradition of *mālama ʻaina*."

Auntie Mili did a quick spin and tossed me an orange.

"We need to feed good microbes in our gut just like we need to feed good microbes in the soil! Have you heard the expression, 'you are what you eat'? The food you eat becomes your body. If you want a junk body, eat junk food. If you want a body that's a clean, self-healing machine, then feed it with foods found in nature, not in factories.

"Whole plant foods contain lots of water and *fiber*. They help you feel full when you eat them, so you can eat all you want. You won't have to count carbs or calories. Your cravings for junk food will disappear. Your taste buds will change, and the food will taste scrumptious. Mark my words!"

"Eat just plants? Sounds a bit extreme," Mom said.

"Extreme compared with what?" asked Auntie Mili. "Going blind? Dropping dead from a stroke? Having a doctor cut off your legs?"

I listened in silence, but my brain was buzzing. Sticking myself with pins and needles and taking medicine for the rest of my life—wasn't *that* extreme?

I felt confused, but also determined. I gave Auntie Mili a giant hug. "If doing this can make me well, then I want to do it with all my heart!"

That night I almost couldn't sleep knowing that maybe the cure for diabetes was sitting right in my living room and at the farm stand. And I knew that no matter what, these foods would not harm me, as some of the drugs might.

Mom suggested we make this an adventure. "Let's have fun learning about as many plant foods as we can, from growing them to cooking them," she said.

We started a garden, and every time we went to the grocery store we bought a fruit or vegetable we had never tried before. We chose a meal plan with lots of colorful veggies, fresh fruit, and leafy greens—who knew there were so many different kinds! We ate many types of beans, peas, lentils, and whole grains, and also squashes, sweet potatoes, and a small amount of nuts and seeds. Most of these foods I was tasting for the first time.

Instead of eating eggs and bacon for breakfast, we ate oatmeal with cinnamon and vanilla, topped with berries. It tasted great! And did you know that vanilla comes from the bean pod of a beautiful orchid? Or that cinnamon comes from the bark of a tree, and can lower blood pressure?

Lavender Oatmeal

3½ Cups water
½ teaspoon cinnamon
¼ teaspoon nutmeg or allspice (or ⅛ t each)
1½ Cups "old fashioned" rolled oats
½ Cup blueberries
½ Cup diced apples
1 teaspoon vanilla
2 Tablespoons chopped walnuts (optional)

Add water and spices to a pot and bring to boil. Stir in oats and return to boil. Reduce heat to simmer and cook about 5 minutes, stirring occasionally. Stir in fruit, vanilla, and walnuts. Heat through, and serve. Yum!

Every day we varied our ingredients. We never got bored because the tastes and colors in our meals were always different.

For lunch, instead of a sandwich with turkey, low-fat cheese, and fat-free mayo, we made thick, chunky soups that were bursting with flavor. We ate giant, crispy salads spiced with herbs we grew in our garden: basil, parsley, chives and mint.

For dinner, we sometimes made dishes with flavors from around the world. Mexican black bean soup, African chickpea stew, Thai vegetable curry, and Indian split-pea dahl were part of our growing collection of recipes. We made enough for leftovers, so we didn't need to cook every day. We came to love these different flavors and to feel *aloha* for the cultures and people who created these dishes.

We shopped at farmers markets and we learned to buy local foods that were fresh, inexpensive, and grown in organic soil. We looked forward to our time in the kitchen, which was always fun. And the food was beautiful to look at, because we were using colors from nature. On days when we felt like eating something simple, we made meals that were fast and easy, such as colorful confetti salad with a side of beans, or boiled *taro* root with a pile of steamed greens.

Taro, or *kalo*, is an interesting food. In Hawaiian culture, kalo is the *staff of life*, and also a spiritual older brother to the Hawaiian people. We had fun visiting a taro farm, where we saw how taro is grown and made into *poi* in the traditional way.

We went to other organic farms, too, and on each visit we learned something new. When we visited farmer Kaiʻs organic farm we saw a giant yellow sign as we turned into the driveway.

The giant yellow welcome sign seemed to say it all, but farmer Kai taught us more. He told us that soil is alive, and it needs to be nourished in the same way that we need to be nourished—with foods that come from the earth. When we use chemicals to kill pests and weeds, these chemicals take life from the soil, and they also end up in our food and in our bodies. This has led to problems for ourselves and the planet. But it's not too late to do something about this. There is a solution if we all work together. *Regenerative farming* turns lifeless dirt back into living soil that is rich in nutrients and free of harmful chemicals. When we eat organic foods grown in living soil, our food becomes the medicine we need to thrive.

Farmer Kai said farming methods that rely on chemicals to grow food have damaged the living systems that keep Earth's climate, land, and oceans in balance. Now Earth's climate is in big trouble. But through regenerative farming we can help Earth's climate come back into balance.

We started calling this Our Great Food Adventure. Who knew that growing healthy food could help us and the planet in so many ways!

Just one week into Our Great Food Adventure the doctor took me off diabetes pills. With each passing week, my weight went down. My mind got clearer, my allergies vanished, and my energy soared.

Mom noticed changes in her body, too. She was twenty pounds lighter and said she felt ten years younger. "Energy up, pounds down, joint aches gone," she laughed.

When I had my three-month checkup, the doctor almost jumped with joy—my blood tests showed my diabetes was *gone*!

"Told ya," Auntie Mili chuckled, beaming.

Mom hugged me and said, "I've got my healthy girl back."

And I got my life back. In fact, I got a *new* life!

When it came time for Auntie Mili to leave, I had no words to thank her for all that she'd done. I just held her tight for a long time and tried to keep my wet cheeks off her silky blue jacket.

As Mom hugged Auntie Mili goodbye, she said, "All my life I've been blaming our genes, when our food and lifestyle are what turns those genes on and off! We all have a few bad genes of some kind, but bad genes can't hurt us when they're turned off. I sure wish I'd known this a long time ago."

Auntie Mili was right. My taste buds changed. I could now taste and enjoy the sweetness of real whole foods. And best of all, my food cravings vanished.

Changing my food habits wasn't all easy, especially in the beginning. It took several weeks, but one day I noticed that the sweet, fatty, salty foods I used to crave had lost their power to grab me. That was huge!

Another amazing thing I discovered was that Mom and I had such fun together experiencing new foods. We learned how much we both love to cook and garden, try new recipes, and shop for fresh foods. We found out how fun it is to spend time together doing things we both enjoy.

Now that I'm grown with two little boys of my own, I nourish them with wholesome, plant-based meals. My children are building fond memories of the foods that make them feel cared for and loved. With these healthy foods, we are making new family traditions of meals we love to eat and look forward to sharing. My boys are learning to garden and cook, to care for their bodies, and to nourish the land that feeds them. They are living the *aloha spirit* and practicing the time-honored values of *aloha* and *mālama 'aina*. They want to become regenerative farmers, and to stand with others around the world who are helping to regenerate planet Earth.

Lessons from Mili

I used to think:
Type 2 diabetes was incurable.
But now I've learned:
Type 2 diabetes can be cured by eating the right foods.

I used to think:
Every disease has a different cause and needs a different treatment.
But now I've learned:
Many chronic diseases—including heart disease, high blood pressure, cancers, and diabetes —are fueled by eating unhealthy foods, and can be prevented and reversed by eating a diet of whole (unprocessed) plant foods.

I used to think:
We needed meat to build strong muscles and milk to build strong bones.
But now I've learned:
We don't need either one. The biggest, strongest animals on earth build their muscles and bones on a diet of plants. A growing number of world-class athletes have switched to eating only whole foods from plants because they find it gives them the winning edge.

I used to think:
Animal foods, such as milk, eggs, cheese, beef, chicken, and fish, were safe and important foods for building health.
But now I've learned:
Eating too much of these foods can make us fat and sick. We can get all the nutrition we need more safely from eating plants.

I used to think:
Eating sweets, sodas, and refined foods couldn't be so bad because "everybody does it," and "they wouldn't sell it to us if it really made us sick."
But now I've learned:
There are many reasons why popular foods may not be healthy, and why popular information may not be true. We must learn to question and think for ourselves.

I used to think:
I would feel hungry, unsatisfied, and weak from eating just plants.
But now I've learned:
Eating plants is delicious and satisfying, and I have *more* energy, not less.

My mom said she used to think:
Life wouldn't be worth living if she had to give up the unhealthy foods she loved, but because of me she was willing to try.

Now she says:
Taste buds *do* change! Healthy foods taste great, make her body feel really good, and make her life more joyful than she ever imagined.

My mom said she used to think:
The way we prepare food doesn't affect its nutrition.
Now she says:
Some cooking methods are healthier than others. Lightly steaming vegetables and gently simmering soups and stews are better than boiling vegetables and pouring off the liquid. Baking without browning and warm-air drying are healthier choices than hot grilling and broiling, which scorch the food. Steam frying is a healthy replacement for frying with oil.

Glossary

aloha: A word used to express greetings, farewells, welcome, and love. More than a word, *aloha* is an overarching spiritual principle that includes living by principles of kindness, harmony, gentleness, humility, and patience.

aloha spirit (spirit of aloha): An attitude or way of life in which mind and heart are aligned to think, feel, and express good feelings to others. *Aloha spirit* recognizes a single life force, shared by all.

compost: Plant fertilizer made from decomposed scraps of living material, such as food scraps, leaves, and grass clippings.

fiber (dietary fiber): The parts of plant foods that are indigestible, but are nevertheless important for our good health. Fiber is important food for good microbes in our gut.

food addiction: An eating behavior that you cannot control even though you know it can harm you.

genes: Small units of information that carry specific information about the body from parents to offspring. Each gene is like a book with many instructions. Which instructions are expressed, and how they are expressed, depends on the environment surrounding the genes.

insulin: A hormone produced by beta cells in the pancreas that lowers the level of sugar in the blood by moving sugar into the cells, where it can be used for energy.

mālama ʻaina: A Hawaiian phrase that means to care for and nurture (mālama) the land (ʻaina) so it can give back what we need to sustain life for ourselves and future generations.

Maui: One of the inhabited islands in the state of Hawaii.

microbes: Bacteria, fungi, and other tiny living organisms that are too small to be seen by the naked eye.

organic: Organic materials come from materials that were once living. Organic soil is rich in nutrients from compost, and also free of added synthetic chemicals.

poi: A traditional Hawaiian food made by pounding taro root and fermenting it to form a sour paste.

processed foods: Foods that have been changed from their natural state. Typically, processed foods are packaged in boxes, bags, bottles, cans, or jars.

shelf life: The length of time a processed food will last before it becomes unfit to eat or sell.

staff of life: A food that is central, or foundational, to one's diet.

taro: A nutritious food plant that grows throughout the tropics. All parts of the taro plant are edible when cooked.

regenerative farming (**regenerative agriculture**): A healthy way of farming that was once traditional before it was replaced by modern chemical-based farming methods.

tutu: The Hawaiian word for grandparent. Tutu *wahine* means grandmother. Tutu *kane* means grandfather.

whole foods: Foods that are still in their naturall state with all their nutritious parts intact. Whole foods may be raw, chopped, or cooked, but they have not been refined, processed, or stripped of their nutrition.

whole food plant-based: A meal or eating style that is composed primarily of plants in their original, unprocessed state.

For Parents and Teachers

A growing body of evidence-based research has demonstrated the remarkable power of food to prevent and cure many chronic diseases, including diabetes, heart disease, multiple sclerosis, arthritis, many cancers, and auto-immune diseases. By educating children about the relationship between diet and disease we provide them with access to lifesaving information and help them establish healthful habits moving forward.

If you want to learn more about the amazing connections between food and our health and how to put this knowledge to practice in your life, please visit the following authors' websites, where you will find their books and DVDS. Many of these websites also host a wealth of free information that includes kitchen tips and recipes, personal success stories, support communities, newsletters, articles, and medical information. Websites were current as of the date of this book's publication.

Neal D. Barnard, MD; www.pcrm.org

T. Colin Campbell, PhD; nutritionstudies.org

Caldwell B. Esselstyn, Jr, MD; dresselstyn.com

Michael Greger, MD; nutritionfacts.org

John McDougall, MD; www.drmcdougall.com

Terry Shintani, MD, JD, MPH; www.drshintani.com

About the Authors

Antonia Demas (PhD Cornell University) is founder and director of Food Studies Institute, a nonprofit organization devoted to educating children and adults in food literacy. Antonia loves working with children and communities to teach them the joys of growing, cooking, and learning about healthy foods of the world. Her food-based curricular programs incorporate a research strategy that scientifically demonstrates the positive impact of food education on student health, behavior, and academic performance. Antonia's vision is to put a food literacy educator into every school in the nation.

Katherine Orr (MS, University of Connecticut) is a scientist and artist who wears many hats. Katherine did field research in the West Indies as a marine biologist for many years. She has authored and illustrated twenty books, mostly for children, and she is an advocate of plant-based nutrition and the many diverse benefits it brings to people, societies, the environment, and the planet.

Katherine and Antonia met in 2015 after Katherine took T. Colin Campbell's eCornell program where Antonia was a guest lecturer. They discovered that they both share a passion for the unique abilities of children, a love of art, and an intense appreciation of nature. Both were born in 1950, exactly one month apart. Though Katherine lives in Hawaii and Antonia lives in the Finger Lakes Region of New York, they collaborated on this book with the hope that it will inspire children to eat foods that will prevent disease and promote the health of people and the planet. Our future depends on it.

We do not inherit the earth from our ancestors, we borrow it from our children.
– Native American Proverb

www.ingramcontent.com/pod-product-compliance
Lightning Source LLC
Chambersburg PA
CBHW042247100526
44587CB00002B/56